PRIMER LEVEL

30 note spelling lessons

By David Carr Glover

David Carr Glover
PIANO LIBRARY

MW00563000

FOREWORD

These 30 NOTE SPELLING LESSONS are for the reinforcement of the music fundamentals found in Primer Level of the David Carr Glover Piano Library. They present note spelling and music fundamentals used at this level of study.

For further reinforcement of music fundamentals at this level of study the following music games published by Belwin-Mills Publishing Corp., created by Helen Wunnenberg and David Carr Glover are recommended. They are: Music Forte (Music Bingo), Music Match - Go, and Music Cross - Go.

CONTENTS

© 1979 BELWIN-MILLS PUBLISHING CORP.
All Rights Administered by WARNER BROS. PUBLICATIONS U.S. INC.
All Rights Reserved including Public Performance for Profit

LESSON No. 1 - Line And Space Notes

This ─⊕─ is a LINE note.

Draw six LINE notes like the one above.

── ────   ──── ────   ──── ────   ──── ────   ──── ────   ──── ──

This ⊐O⊏ is a SPACE note.

Draw six SPACE notes like the one above.

═══   ═══   ═══   ═══   ═══   ═══

Notes are placed on a STAFF.

Mark an X under all LINE notes.

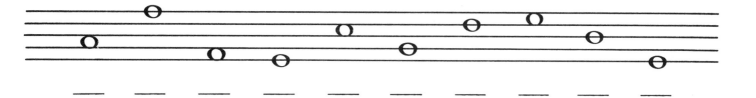

Mark an X under all SPACE notes.

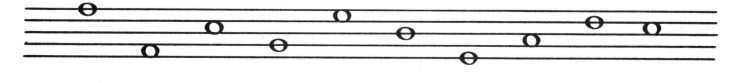

FDL 767

© 1979 BELWIN-MILLS PUBLISHING CORP.
All Rights Administered by WARNER BROS. PUBLICATIONS U.S. INC.
All Rights Reserved including Public Performance for Profit

LESSON No. 2 - Identifying Line And Space Notes

On the staffs below are line and space notes. Write L for LINE notes and S for SPACE notes.

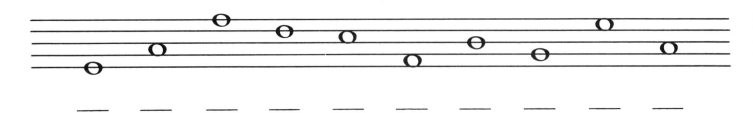

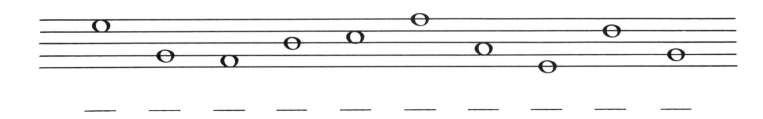

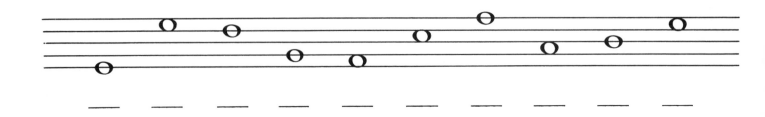

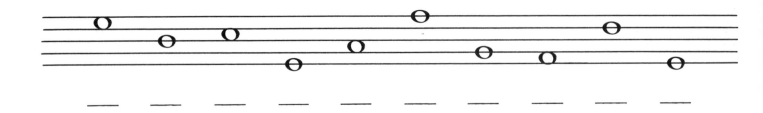

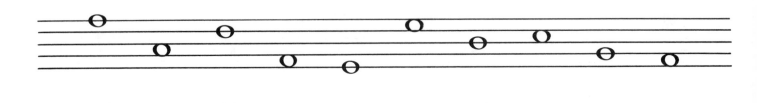

LESSON No. 3 - Line Number Names

The music staff has FIVE lines.

They are numbered from the bottom to the top.

Number the lines on the staff below.

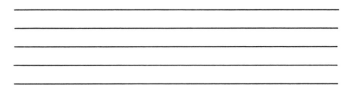

Counting from the bottom up to the top write the number names for the LINE notes below.

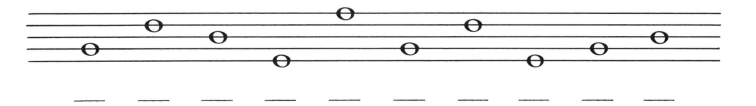

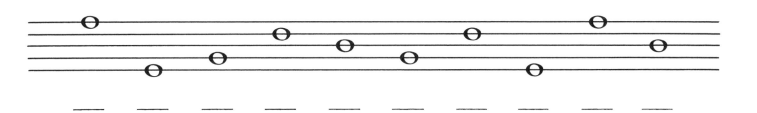

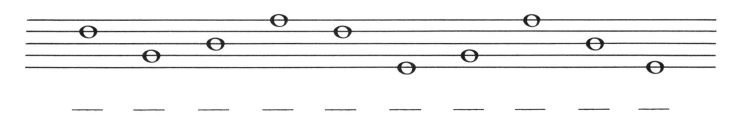

LESSON No. 4 - Space Number Names

The music staff has FOUR spaces.

They are numbered from the bottom to the top.

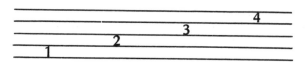

Number the spaces on the staff below.

Counting from the bottom up to the top write the number names for the SPACE notes below.

LESSON No. 5 - Drawing Whole Notes On Line And Spaces

Using Whole Notes draw LINE notes indicated. Count from the bottom up to the top.

| 3 | 2 | 1 | 4 | 5 | 2 | 1 | 3 | 5 | 4 |

| 4 | 5 | 3 | 1 | 2 | 5 | 4 | 1 | 2 | 3 |

Using Whole Notes draw SPACE notes indicated. Count from the bottom up to the top.

| 1 | 4 | 2 | 3 | 2 | 4 | 1 | 3 | 2 | 4 |

| 4 | 2 | 3 | 1 | 4 | 2 | 3 | 2 | 4 | 1 |

Using Whole Notes draw the LINE and SPACE notes indicated. Count from the bottom up to the top.

| 5L | 1S | 1L | 3L | 2S | 2L | 3S | 4L | 4S | 1L |

LESSON No. 6 - Music Alphabet Letter Names

The Music Alphabet uses the following letter names:

A B C D E F G

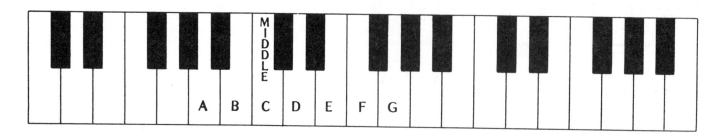

How many letters are there in the Music Alphabet? _____

In the correct order they are: _____

Fill in the missing letter names for the following Music Alphabets.

1. __A__ ____ __C__ __D__ ____ __F__ __G__

2. __A__ __B__ ____ __D__ ____ __F__ ____

3. ____ __B__ __C__ ____ __E__ ____ __G__

4. __A__ ____ ____ __D__ ____ __F__ ____

5. ____ ____ __C__ ____ __E__ ____ __G__

LESSON No. 7 - White Key Letter Names

The Music Alphabet is repeated over and over again on the white keys of the keyboard.

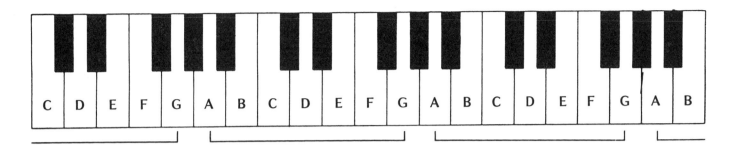

On the following white keys write letter names to complete the two Music Alphabets. The first letter name is given for each.

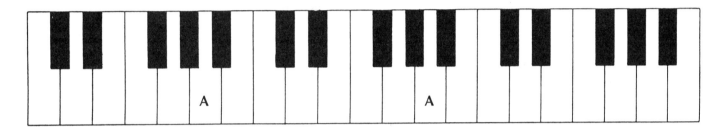

Write the letter names for the Music Alphabet forward below.

_____ _____ _____ _____ _____ _____ _____

Write the letter names for the Music Alphabet backwards below.

_____ _____ _____ _____ _____ _____ _____

Fill in the missing letter names for the following Music Alphabet.

_____ B _____ D _____ F _____

LESSON No. 8 - Identifying White Keys

Write the letter C on all white C keys.

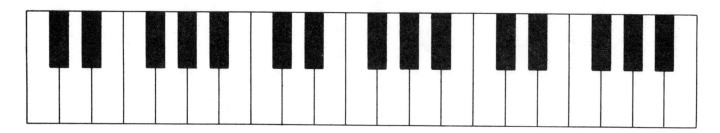

Write the letter A on all white A keys.

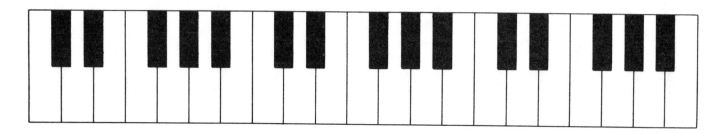

Write the letter G on all white G keys.

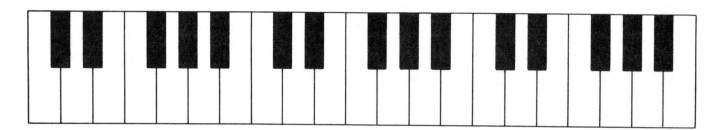

Write the letter B on all white B keys.

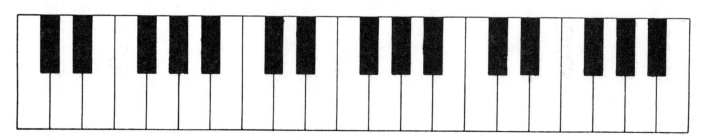

LESSON No. 9 - Identifying White Keys

Write the letter D on all white D keys.

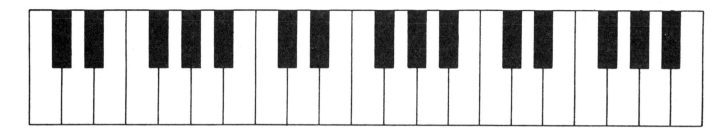

Write the letter F on all white F keys.

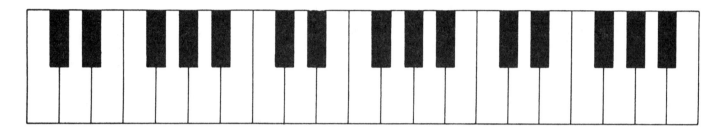

Write the letter E on all white E keys.

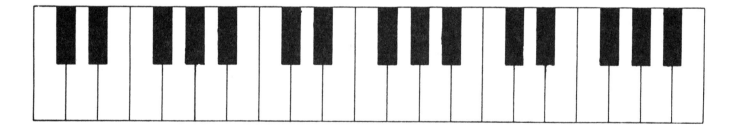

Write the letter A on all white A keys.

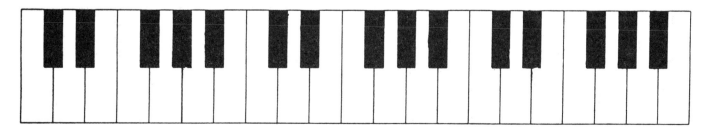

FDL 767

LESSON No. 10 - White Key Spelling

Write letter names on all white keys marked with an X.

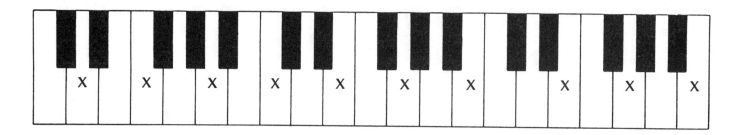

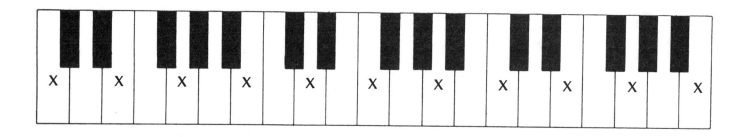

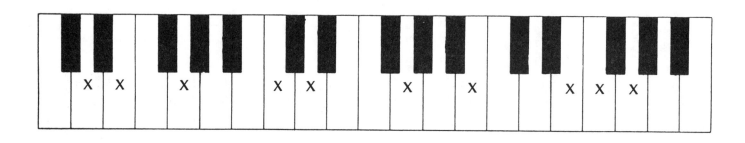

LESSON No. 11 - Drawing Clef Signs

This 𝄞 is a Treble or G Clef sign. When it is placed at the beginning of a staff it creates a Treble Staff.

Trace the following five steps to create a Treble Clef sign.

Draw ten complete Treble Clef signs below.

This 𝄢 is a Bass or F Clef sign. When it is placed at the beginning of a staff it creates a Bass Staff.

Trace the following four steps to create a Bass Clef sign.

Draw eight complete Bass Clef signs below.

FDL 767

LESSON No. 12 - Creating The Grand Staff

When a Treble Staff and Bass Staff are joined together with a Brace and Bar Line a Grand Staff is created.

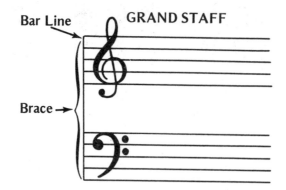

Complete nine Grand Staffs below.

LESSON No. 13 - The Notes Of Middle C-D-E On Treble Staff

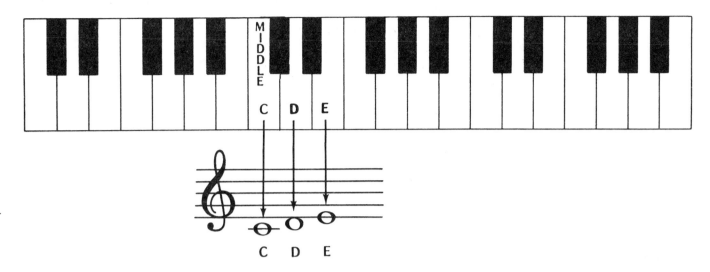

Write the correct letter names for the following Treble Staff notes.

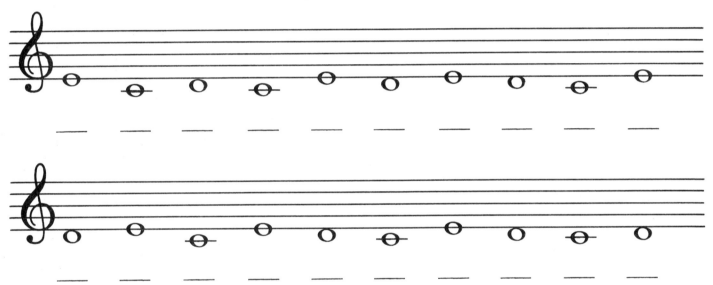

Using the above key-note guide draw the correct Treble Staff notes above the given letter names. Use whole notes.

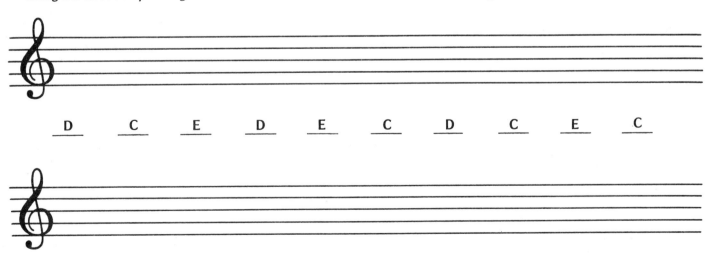

D   C   E   D   E   C   D   C   E   C

E   D   C   C   E   D   E   C   D   E

FDL 767

LESSON No. 14 - The Notes Of A-B-Middle C On Bass Staff

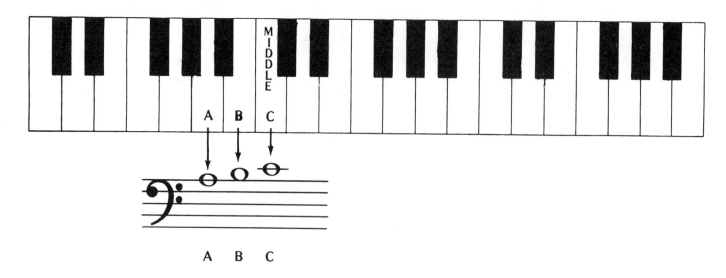

Write the correct letter names for the following Bass Staff notes.

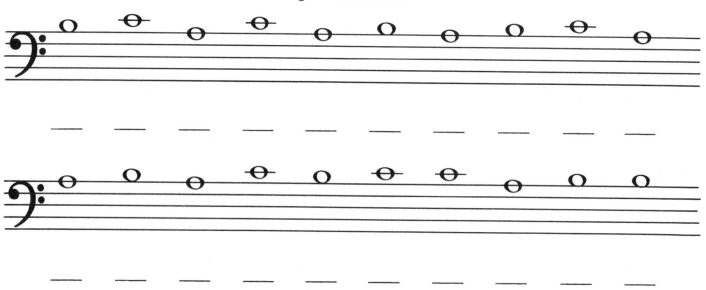

Using the above key-note guide draw the correct Bass Staff notes above the given letter names. Use whole notes.

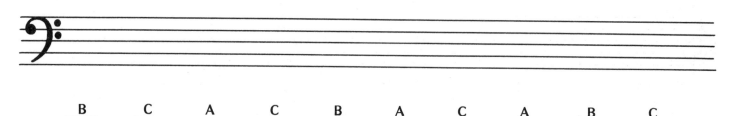

B   C   A   C   B   A   C   A   B   C

A   C   B   C   A   B   C   B   A   B

LESSON No. 15 - The Notes Of Middle C-D-E-F On Treble Staff

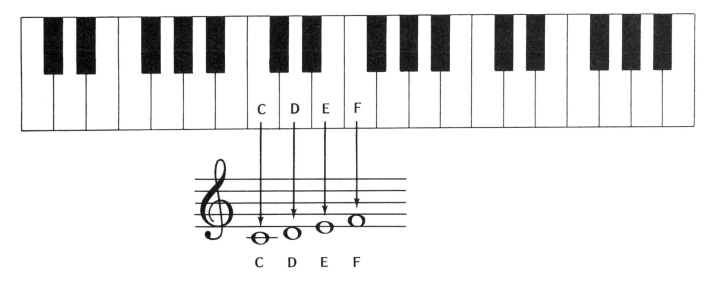

Write the correct letter names for the following Treble Staff notes.

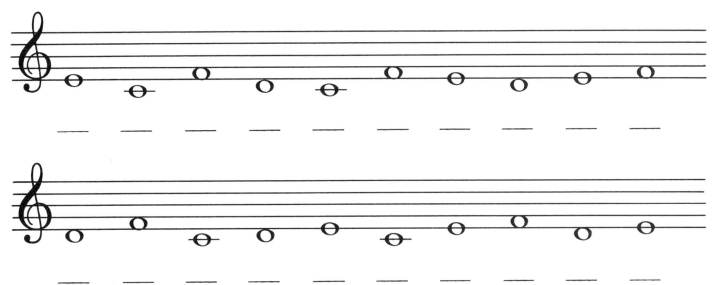

Using the above key-note guide draw the correct Treble Staff notes above the given letter names. Use whole notes.

F   D   C   E   C   F   D   E   F   C

C   F   D   E   F   D   E   C   F   D

LESSON No. 16 - The Notes Of G-A-B-Middle C On Bass Staff

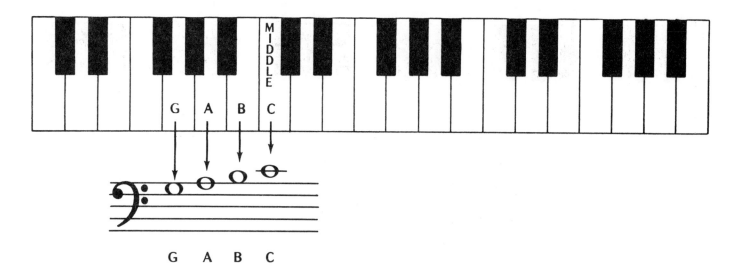

Write the correct letter names for the following Bass Staff notes.

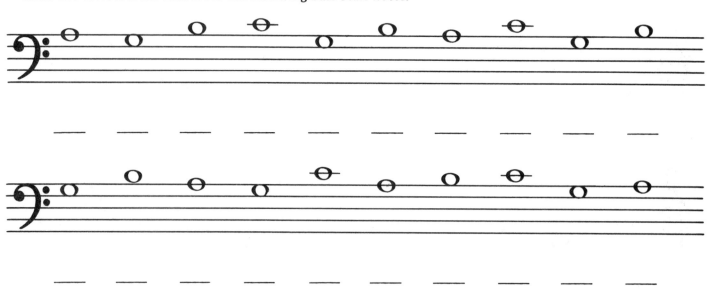

Using the above key-note guide draw the correct Bass Staff notes above the given letter names. Use whole notes.

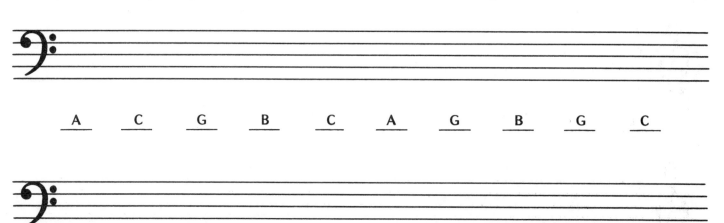

A   C   G   B   C   A   G   B   G   C

G   C   A   B   C   G   B   A   C   G

LESSON No. 17 - The Notes Of Middle C-D-E-F-G On Treble Staff

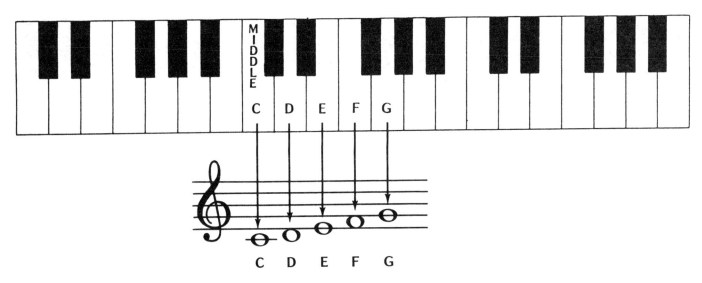

Write the correct letter names for the following Treble Staff notes.

Using the above key-note guide draw the correct Treble Staff notes above the given letter names. Use whole notes.

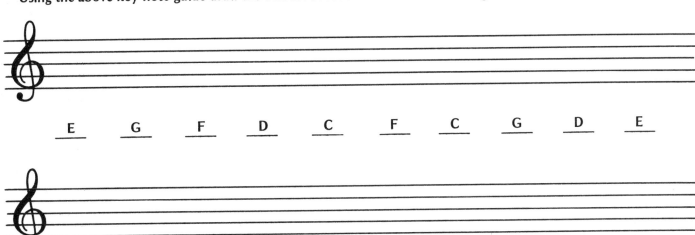

E   G   F   D   C   F   C   G   D   E

G   D   F   E   C   D   F   G   C   G

FDL 767

LESSON No. 18 - The Notes Of F-G-A-B-Middle C On Bass Staff

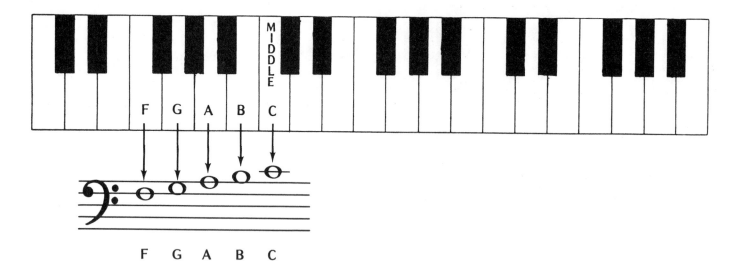

Write the correct letter names for the following Bass Staff notes.

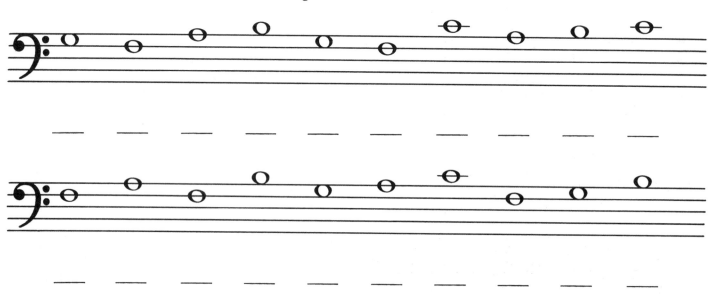

Using the above key-note guide draw the correct Bass Staff notes above the given letter names. Use whole notes.

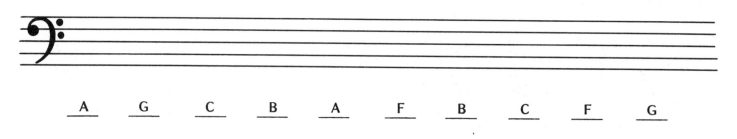

A   G   C   B   A   F   B   C   F   G

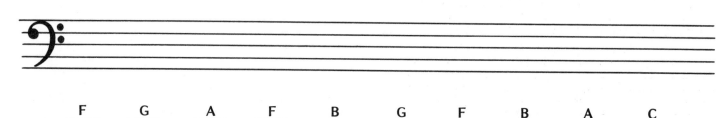

F   G   A   F   B   G   F   B   A   C

FDL 767

LESSON No. 19 - Kinds Of Notes And Stem Placement

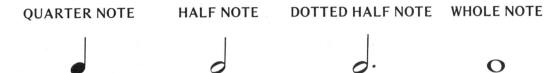

QUARTER NOTE · · · · HALF NOTE · · · DOTTED HALF NOTE · · WHOLE NOTE

All notes, except whole notes, have stems. Up stems are on the <u>right</u> side of a note. Draw up stems for the following notes.

Down stems are on the <u>left</u> side of a note. Draw down stems for the following notes.

When the note is on or above the middle line of the staff the stem goes down on the left.

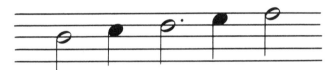

When the note is below the middle line of the staff the stem goes up on the right.

Change the following note heads to Quarter Notes.

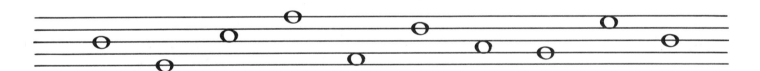

Change the following note heads to Half Notes.

Change the following note heads to Dotted Half Notes.

FDL 767

LESSON No. 20 - Note Spelling Grand Staff

Write the correct letter names for the following Grand Staff notes. They spell words.

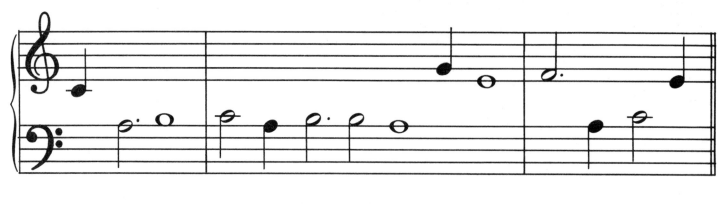

— — — — — — — — — — — —

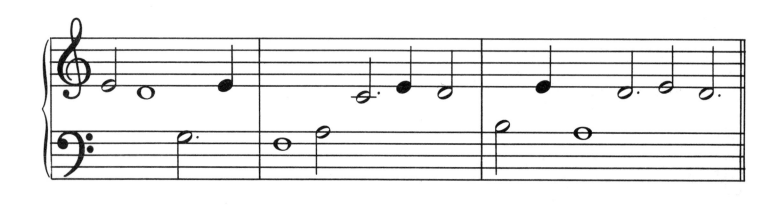

— — — — — — — — — — — — — —

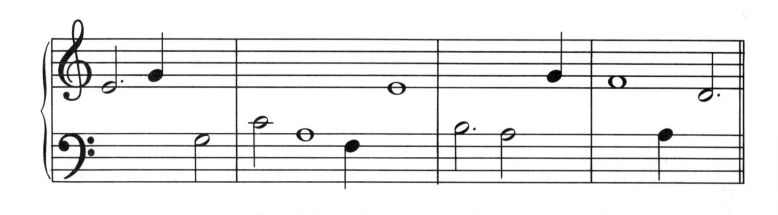

— — — — — — — — — — — — — — —

— — — — — — — — — — — — — — —

FDL 767

LESSON No. 21 - Sharps

This 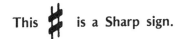 is a Sharp sign.

On a music staff it may appear in a space

or with a line through it.

Trace the following sharp signs.

Draw a Sharp sign in front of the following notes.

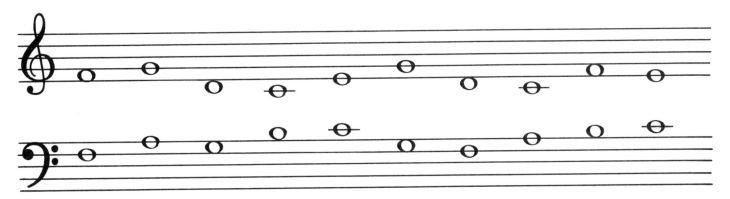

Write the correct letter names for the following Sharp signs.

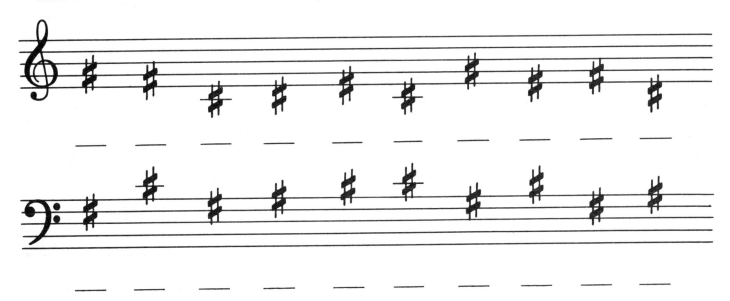

FDL 767

LESSON No. 22 - Flats

This ♭ is a Flat sign.

On a music staff it may appear in a space

or with a line through it ♭ .

Trace the following flat signs.

Draw a Flat sign in front of the following notes.

Write the correct letter names for the following Flat signs.

FDL 767

LESSON No. 23 - Note Spelling - Key Of G Major

F♯ at the beginning of a piece of music means that all Fs are to be played sharp. F♯ is the Key Signature for the Key of G Major.

Write letter names for the following notes. Be sure to observe the Key Signature.

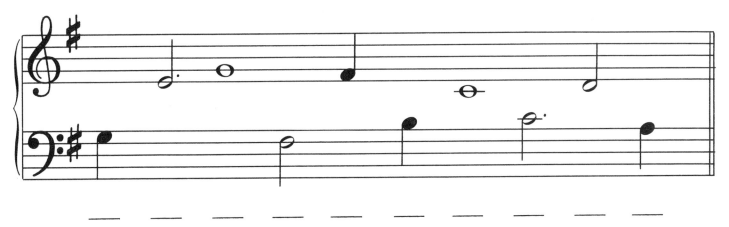

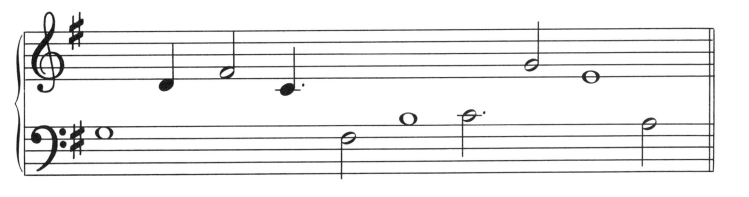

FDL 767

LESSON No. 24 - Note Spelling - Key Of F Major

B♭ at the beginning of a piece of music means all Bs are to be played flat.
B♭ is the Key Signature for the Key of F Major.

Write letter names for the following notes. Be sure to observe the Key Signature.

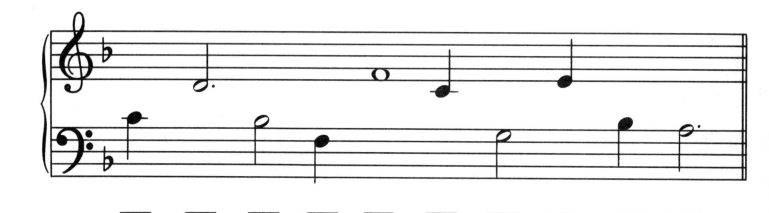

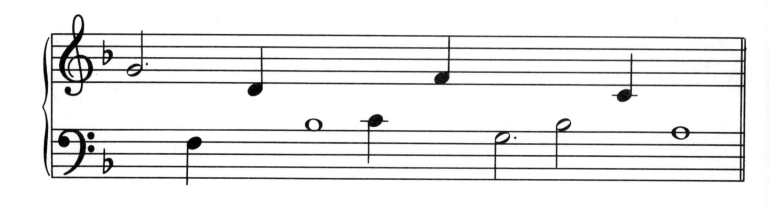

FDL 767

LESSON No. 25 - Note Spelling - Key Of C Major

When there are no sharps or flats at the beginning of a piece of music, the music does not have a Key Signature and it is in the Key of C Major.

Write letter names for the following notes.

FDL 767

LESSON No. 26 - The Notes Of C-D-E-F-G-A-B-Middle C On Bass Staff

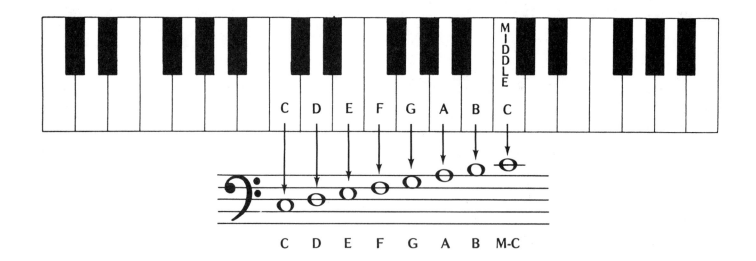

Write the correct letter names for the following Bass Staff notes.

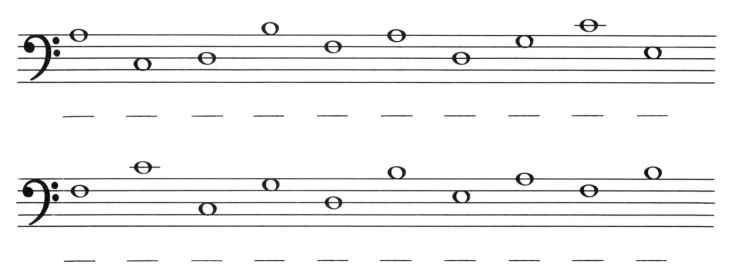

Using the above key-note guide draw the correct Bass Staff notes above the given letter names. Use whole notes. (M-C means Middle C.)

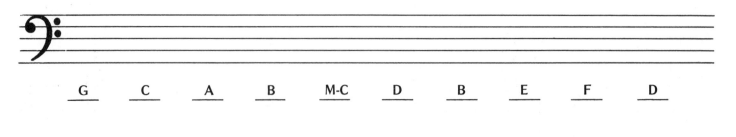

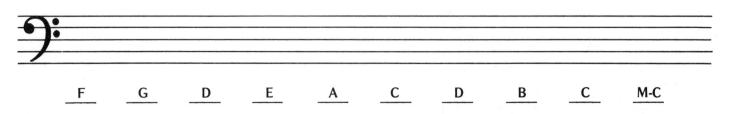

LESSON No. 27 - The Notes Of Middle C-D-E-F-G-A-B-C On Treble Staff

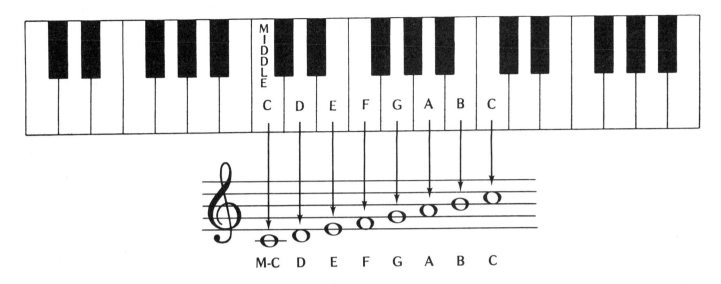

Write the correct letter names for the following Treble Staff notes.

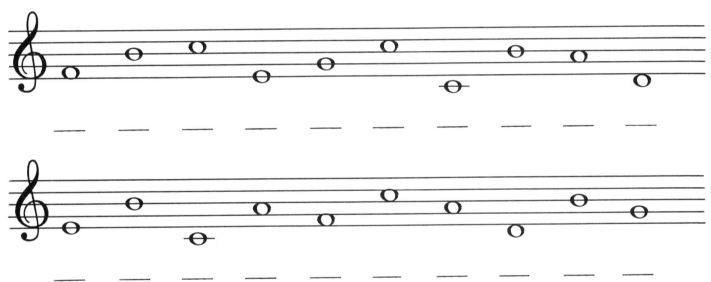

Using the above key-note guide draw the correct Treble Staff notes above the given letter names. Use whole notes. (M-C means Middle C.)

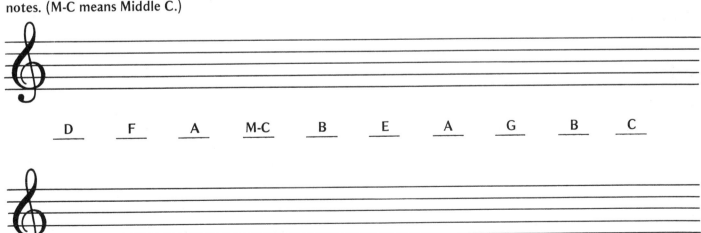

D   F   A   M-C   B   E   A   G   B   C

A   D   B   A   E   G   B   M-C   C   F

LESSON No. 28 - Note Spelling - Keys Of C-F-G Major

Write letter names for the following notes. Be sure to observe the Key Signature.

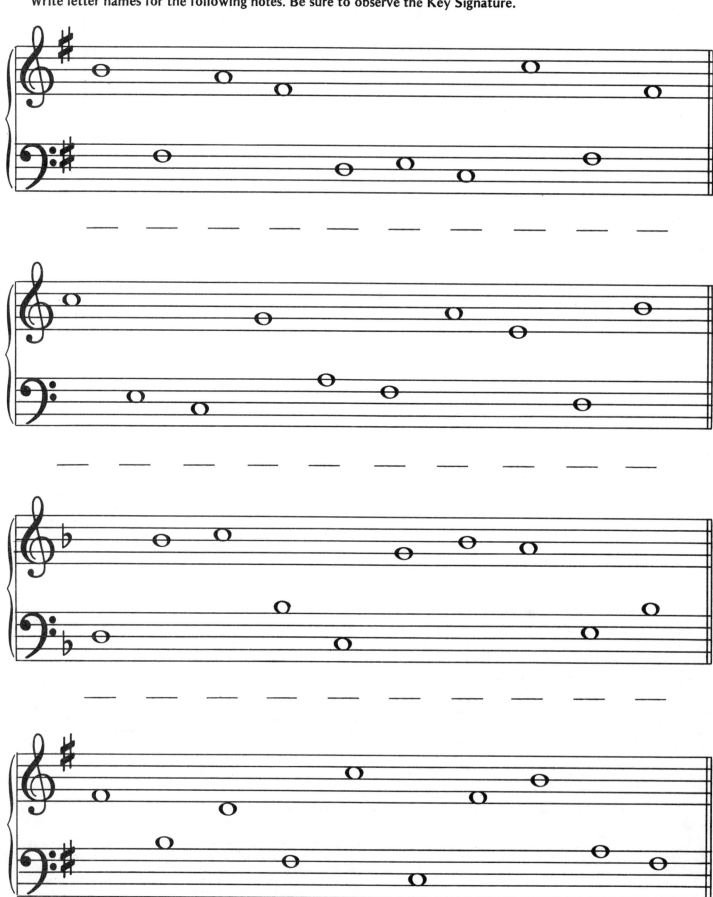

LESSON No. 29 - Identifying Kinds Of Rest

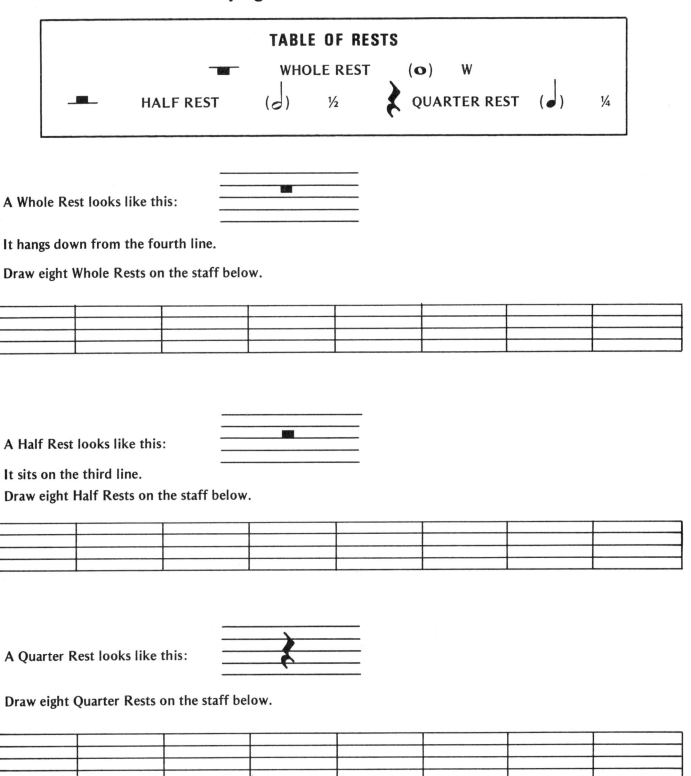

A Whole Rest looks like this:

It hangs down from the fourth line.

Draw eight Whole Rests on the staff below.

A Half Rest looks like this:

It sits on the third line.

Draw eight Half Rests on the staff below.

A Quarter Rest looks like this:

Draw eight Quarter Rests on the staff below.

Identify the following kinds of rests. W = Whole, ½ = Half, ¼ = Quarter.

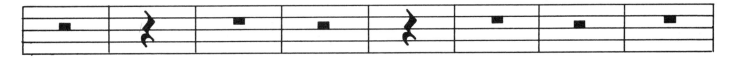

LESSON No. 30 - Drawing Specific Notes

Draw the specific notes indicated.

Use Whole Notes.

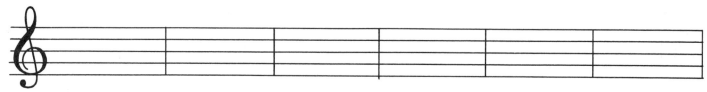

C Space   E Line   C Middle   F Space   G Line   A Space

Use Half Notes.

Middle C   B Space   F Line   C Space   G Space   D Line

Use Quarter Notes.

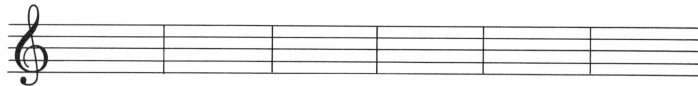

B Line   D Space   C Space   A Space   E Line   G Line

Use Dotted Half Notes.

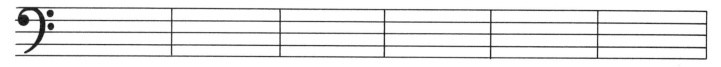

A Line   E Space   C Space   F Line   G Space   B Space

Use Whole Notes.

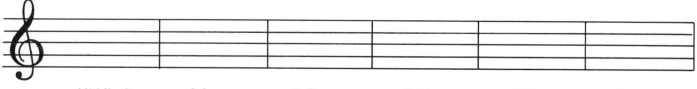

Middle C   C Space   D Space   B Line   G Line   A Space

Use Half Notes

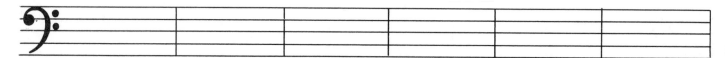

B Space   F Line   C Space   A Line   Middle C   D Line